For Cedric. Thanks for the inspiration.—L.C.-R.

For Malcolm. Endless thanks for all of your hard
work in bringing Pelé to life.—J.E.R.

Text copyright © 2007 by Lesa Cline-Ransome • Cover art and interior illustrations copyright © 2007 by James E. Ransome • All rights
reserved. Published in the United States by Dragonfly Books, an imprint of Random House Children's Books, a division of Random House,
Inc., New York. Originally published in hardcover in the United States by Schwartz & Wade Books, an imprint of Random House Children's
Books, New York, in 2007. • Dragonfly Books with the colophon is a registered trademark of Random House, Inc. • Visit us on the Web!
www.randomhouse.com/kids • Educators and librarians, for a variety of teaching tools, visit us at www.randomhouse.com/teachers
The Library of Congress has cataloged the hardcover edition of this work as follows: Cline-Ransome, Lesa. • Young Pelé: soccer's first star / Lesa
Cline-Ransome ; paintings by James E. Ransome. — 1st ed. • p. cm. • ISBN 978-0-375-83599-5 (trade) — ISBN 978-0-375-93599-2 (lib. bdg.)
[1. Pelé, 1940– —Juvenile literature. 2. Soccer players—Brazil—Biography—Juvenile literature.] I. Ransome, James, ill. II. Title. • GV942.7.P42 C55
2007b 796.334092—dc22 [B] • 2006030840 • ISBN 978-0-375-87156-6 (pbk.)

MANUFACTURED IN CHINA

14

First Dragonfly Books Edition

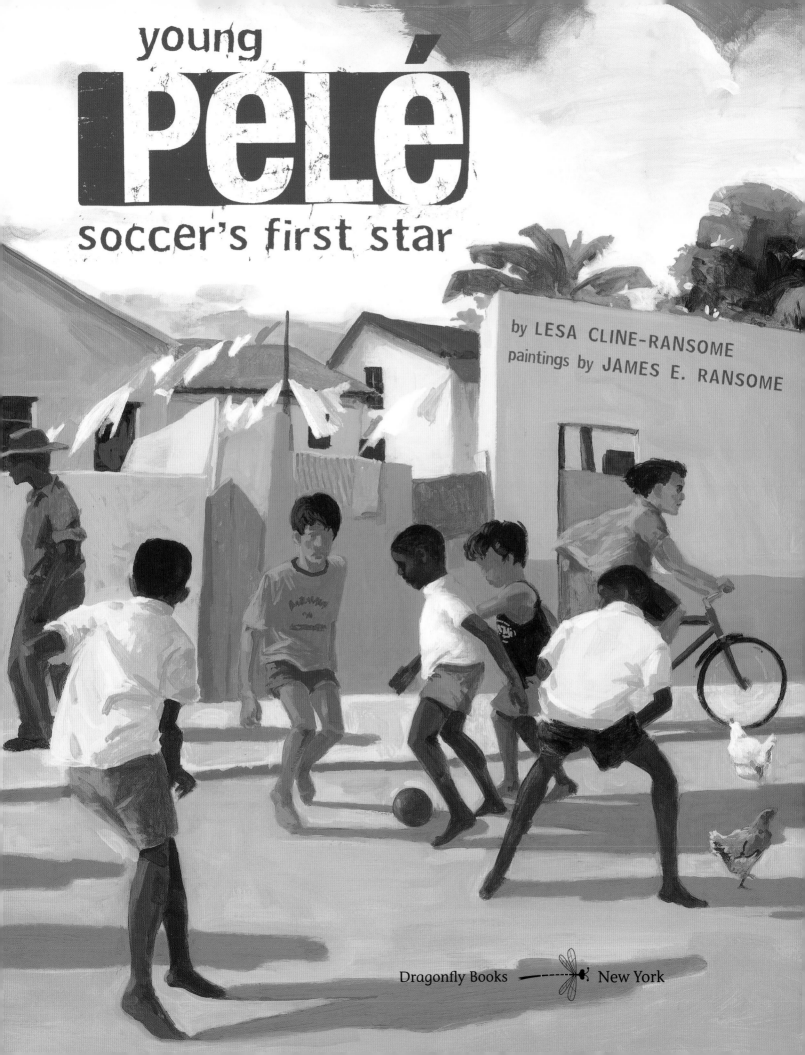

young PELÉ
soccer's first star

by LESA CLINE-RANSOME
paintings by JAMES E. RANSOME

Dragonfly Books -----➤ New York

In a tiny schoolhouse at the edge of the road in Bauru, Brazil, sat a boy with just a hint of a smile on his face. He stared straight ahead at the chalkboard as his teacher spoke, but his mind was miles away.

Though he was the smallest in his class, eight-year-old Edson sat tall at his desk. While others memorized letters, Edson memorized scores from last night's soccer match. While others practiced adding and subtracting, Edson practiced kicking an imaginary soccer ball. And while others heard the teacher calling out numbers and words, Edson heard an announcer calling a game:

With just seconds left, Edson takes the ball. Past one defender and then another. Now he's all alone, only the goalie between him and the goal. "Edson! Edson! Edson!" the fans shout. But Edson stays focused, he bears down, he drives a kick to the right. The ball hits the goalpost, spins back, and flies through the goalie's hands, straight into . . .

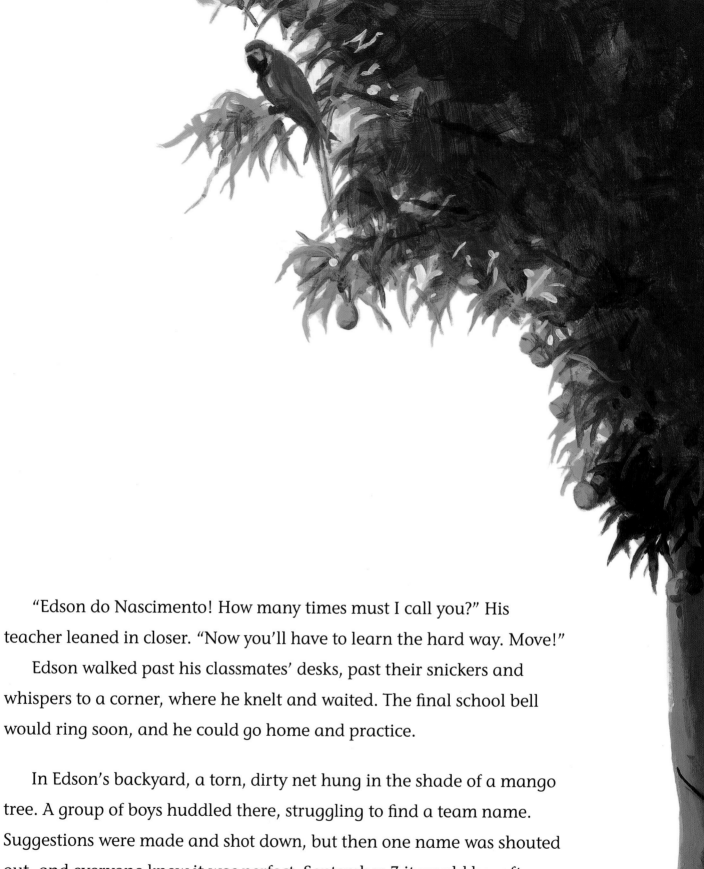

"Edson do Nascimento! How many times must I call you?" His teacher leaned in closer. "Now you'll have to learn the hard way. Move!"

Edson walked past his classmates' desks, past their snickers and whispers to a corner, where he knelt and waited. The final school bell would ring soon, and he could go home and practice.

In Edson's backyard, a torn, dirty net hung in the shade of a mango tree. A group of boys huddled there, struggling to find a team name. Suggestions were made and shot down, but then one name was shouted out, and everyone knew it was perfect. September 7 it would be, after Brazil's national day of independence.

Each afternoon the team practiced in Edson's backyard or along potholed roads and dirt-packed fields, kicking up clouds of dust so thick the players could barely see the ball. As daylight faded, mothers' voices called boys home one by one. "Serginho!" "Nilo!" "Shôde!" "Luisinho!" "Dino!" "Valdo!" "Edson!"

"See you tomorrow!" Edson would shout as he grabbed his ball—a sock stuffed with rags, rolled up, and tied with string. Then he'd head home, tired and happy.

Edson lived with his parents, Dondinho and Dona Celeste; his grandma; and his younger brother and sister. Dondinho had once been a fine soccer player, but a knee injury had destroyed his dream of playing for a pro team. After supper and into the night, he and Edson would listen to matches on the radio, straining to hear the announcers through the static: "Going up . . . across to . . . beautiful kick . . . Goal!"

Dona Celeste stayed away, fussing about the two of them wasting their time.

When Edson finally went to bed, he'd close his eyes, then fast-forward to all the plays he'd try in practice the next day. "If I pass to Nilo, then fake left past Shôde, Nilo can kick a high pass back to me, and I'll head it into the goal. . . ." Too late he'd fall asleep, still clutching his ball of sock and string.

On the way to school every morning Edson liked to kick one rock,

then another, until he was kicking rocks from side to side,

dribbling around people's feet and into potholes—**score!**

When the morning bell rang, his thoughts were so focused on perfecting his plays that he rarely even heard it.

School only got worse. Edson's teachers dreamed up punishments they thought would make him pay attention. For talking in class his mouth was stuffed with paper; for fooling around at his desk he was made to kneel on beans.

Although his parents warned him to behave and punished him when he didn't, Edson soon decided it was easier to skip school altogether— and play soccer.

Around town September 7 became known as the Shoeless Ones, a pretty good team of boys who kicked around a ball of rags and were too poor to afford shoes.

"What about uniforms?" Zé Porto, a defender on the team, wondered one day.

"Yeah, and shoes, too!" everyone agreed, thinking maybe a new look would change their image.

The boys put their heads together and came up with a plan. They would enter contests, shine shoes, sell peanuts.

Soon they'd earned enough to buy shirts, socks, and shorts made from flour sacks.

But they still didn't have enough for shoes.

For Edson and his team, playing the game was all that mattered.
They challenged everyone to take them on—even the locals who
streamed out of the factory at the end of their shifts and stopped to
watch the boys practice.

It wasn't long before older players who had once turned Edson and his friends down were playing against them. And—barefoot—the Shoeless Ones were winning.

It started one day during practice. Someone called him Pelé, then someone else, and someone else—until the entire team was doing it. At first Edson thought they were calling him the name of legendary soccer star Bilé. He didn't like it. But after weeks of hearing "Pelé!" Edson weakened. Maybe a nickname was a good idea—something fans and announcers could shout out. "Edson Arantes do Nascimento" was too long, and anyway, all the best soccer players had nicknames. Why not "Pelé". . . whatever it meant?

The Shoeless Ones had been together for nearly four years when Senhor Nicola Avalone Júnior, the town's mayor, announced he was sponsoring a youth soccer tournament for neighborhood teams who had uniforms and soccer shoes. Now they needed shoes or they couldn't compete.

Zé Leite, a struggling salesman and the father of three of the players, offered his help, and the team gratefully accepted.

Not only did he find them shoes, he agreed to be their new coach. "If you train properly and follow my orders," Zé Leite instructed, "you can win this tournament." And so, almost overnight, the Shoeless Ones disappeared and a new team was born, with a new coach and a new name: Amériquinha, "Little America."

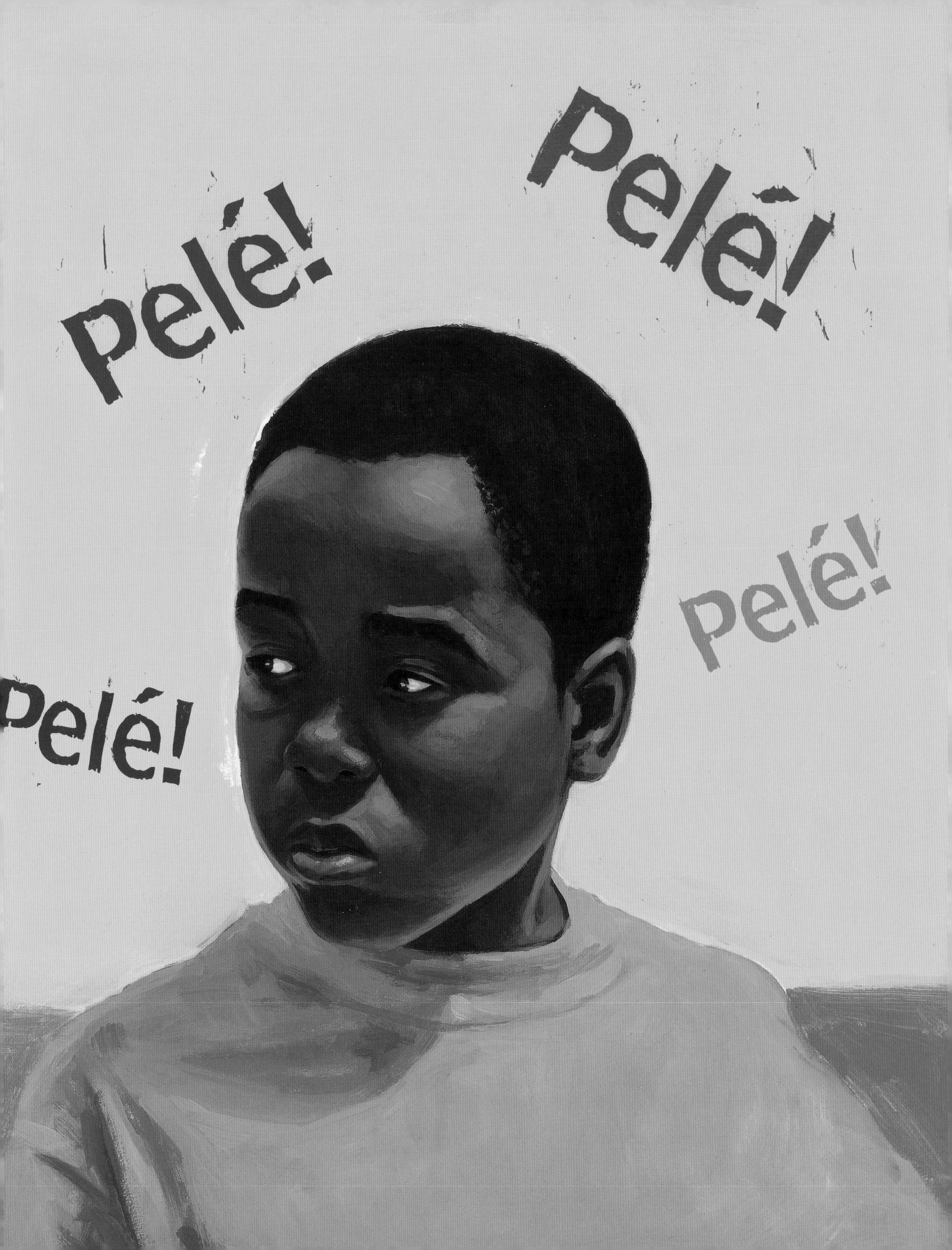
Pelé!
Pelé!
Pelé!
Pelé!

Using his sales skills, Zé Leite got hold of a collection of badly worn soccer shoes, donations from another local team. *"Pé de pobre não tem tamanho,"* he shouted in their native Portuguese as the boys dived for the shoes. "The foot of the poor man doesn't have a size."

Now, instead of focusing on their feet, the team could concentrate on the game . . . though playing *with* shoes took some getting used to.

Between regular practices, twelve-year-old Pelé and his teammates worked on drills Zé Leite designed—leaping, dribbling, heading, trapping, dribbling again—so much, so fast, they could do them without even thinking. Pelé became the unofficial captain because he owned the ball.

And he remained the captain because of all the knowledge he had from talking soccer, listening to soccer, watching and playing soccer with his father.

"Edson, you only know how to use your right foot," Dondinho would warn. "A good player uses each foot equally. And remember, middle of the forehead, eyes open, mouth shut. That's it!" he'd shout as Pelé headed the ball. "All right. Now back to the feet. Left foot, right foot. Like this. That's better. Again."

When they returned home, Dona Celeste was always waiting in the doorway, shaking her head. "Dondinho, don't come complaining to me when he wants to be a soccer player instead of a doctor."

But Dondinho would simply laugh. "Celeste, if he doesn't learn to use his left foot, you have nothing to worry about!"

Pelé's skills were growing faster than his body. By now his teammates were heads taller than Pelé, but it was Pelé who could *play*—center forward, defense, even goalie. Other teams noticed how quickly he dribbled, always with an eye for a pass.

"Gooooaaaaalll!" fans would shout when Pelé scored—usually into a tight corner of the goal, or after a quick fake.

In a game where one goal is often all that's scored, Pelé could score three, alone. Other teams with better uniforms, coaches, and fields tried to convince him to play for them. But Pelé stayed loyal to Amériquinha.

When Amériquinha's turn came to play in the youth soccer tournament, the team knew it had one advantage over all the others: its players could work together.

On the day of their game, the Bauru Athletic Club stadium was packed with five thousand fans. Standing on the lush green grass, Pelé forgot all about his father watching in the stands and his mother worrying at home over his future. "Left foot, right foot," he said to himself, over and over again. By the time the whistle blew, he was focused only on the goal.

The first goal was scored by the opposing team. But Amériquinha stayed cool, playing as one, reading each other's signals as if the team spoke its own secret language—and scored!

Again each team scored. And then Amériquinha caught fire, driving downfield with incredible speed. One quick pass from the right, and . . .